PEGASUS ENCYCLOPEDIA LIBRARY

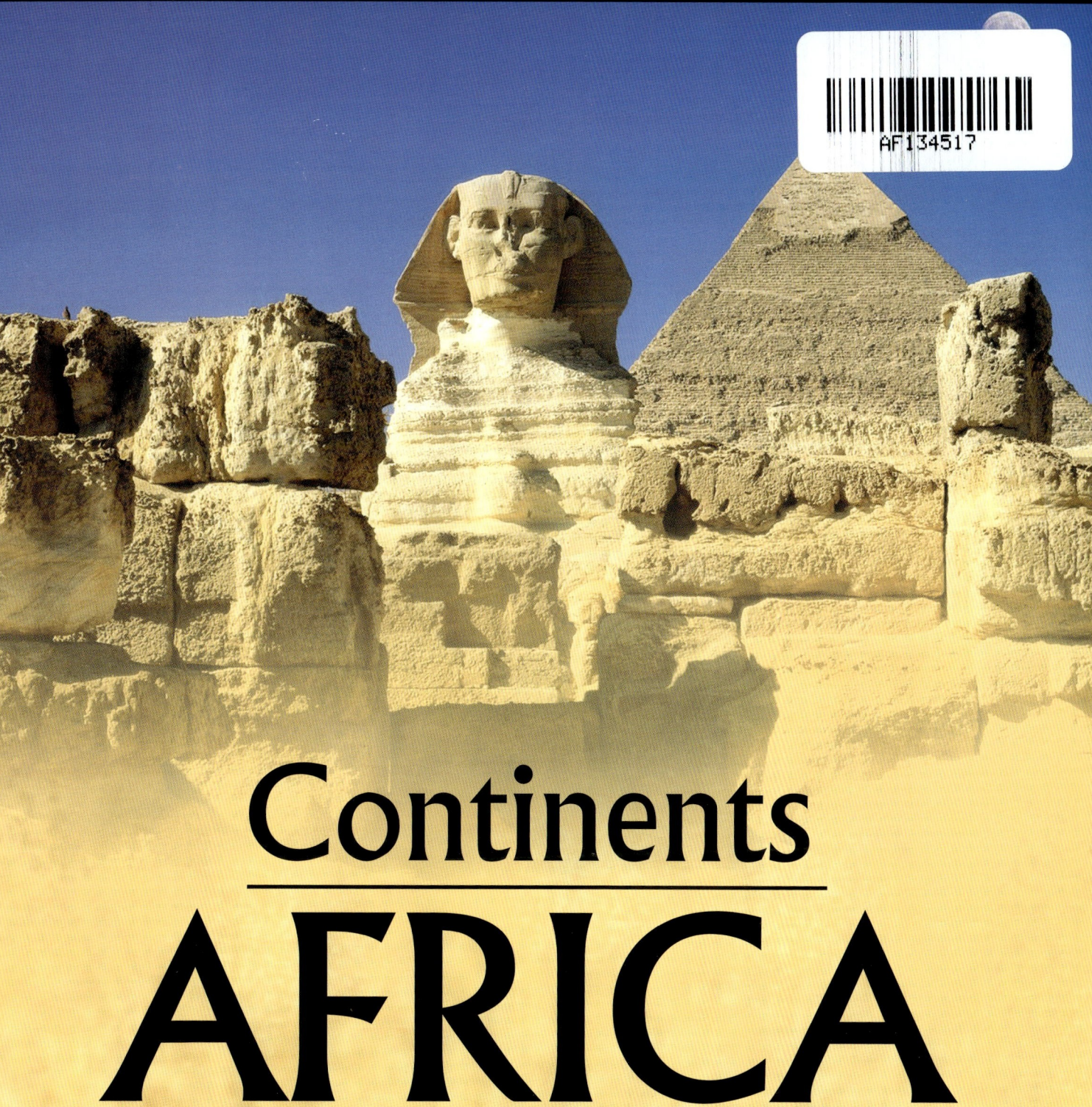

Continents
AFRICA

Edited by: Pallabi B. Tomar, Hitesh Iplani
Managing editor: Tapasi De
Designed by: Vijesh Chahal, Anil Kumar, Rohit Kumar
Illustrated by: Suman S. Roy, Tanoy Choudhury
Colouring done by: Vinay Kumar, Kiran Kumari & Pradeep Kumar

CONTENTS

Introduction 3

Geography 5

Climate 9

History 10

Religion in Africa 17

Festivals 19

Amazing Africa 24

Famous people 30

Test Your Memory 31

Index 32

Introduction

The continent of Africa is the second largest and the second most-populous continent on Earth after Asia. It includes a total number of 57 countries which is more than any other continent. It covers 6 per cent of the Earth's total surface area and 20.4 per cent of the total land area.

The continent spans across the equator and contains numerous climate regions, and is the only continent to stretch from the northern temperate to southern temperate zones (temperate zones are those regions which lie between the tropics and the polar circles.)

Nile River in Africa is the world's longest river system with a length of 6,650 km. Also, Africa is home to the world's largest desert—the Sahara Desert.

AFRICA

The origin of the word **Africa** is still uncertain, but it may have originated from the Latin word 'Africa' which means 'sunny' and from the Greek word 'Aphrike' which means 'not cold'. The Romans were the first to use the name. Another possible source for the name is the name of the first people the Romans met on this continent, the **Afri**, who were a barbaric tribe in the Carthage area.

Mt. Kilimanjaro in Tanzania

Africa at a glance

Area	30, 244, 000 km² (approimately)
Highest point	Mount Kilimanjaro in Tanzania (5, 895 m)
Lowest point	Lake Assal in Djibouti, Horn of Africa (153 m below sea level)
Largest Lake	Lake Victoria; 68, 870 km²
Longest River	Nile; 6, 695 km
Length of coast-line	26, 000 km
Extreme points (including island bodies)	
North	Tunisia
South	Cape Agulhas, South Africa
West	Cape Verde Island
East	Rodrigues, Mauritius
Extreme points (mainland)	
North	Cape Blanc, Tunisia
South	Cape Agulhas, South Africa (approximately 8, 000 km)
West	Cap Vert Peninsula, Senegal
East	Ras Hafun, Somalia (approximately 7,400 km)

Geography

Africa is connected to Asia by the Isthmus of Suez, and separated from Europe by the Mediterranean Sea. Major bodies of water that border the continent are the Mediterranean Sea in the north, the Red Sea in the northeast, the Indian Ocean in the southeast, and the Atlantic Ocean in the west.

The Gulf of Aden is located in the northeast in the Red Sea, the Mozambique Channel lies between Mozambique and the island of Madagascar, and the Gulf of Guinea lies in the west in the Atlantic Ocean.

The prime meridian, the zero degrees longitude which divides the world into Eastern and Western Hemispheres, runs vertically through Africa. The equator, the zero degrees latitude which divides the world into northern and southern hemisphere, runs horizontally through Africa.

AFRICA

Africa is the only continent occupying parts of all the four hemispheres of Earth. Due to a lack of well-defined peninsulas and indentations, the coastline of Africa, which measures some 30,400 km, is almost regular everywhere.

Even though Africa is the second largest continent, it has surprisingly little variety of physical features. Vast plateaus at varying elevations cover the entire continent. Very rarely do these plateaus have rough surfaces. However, the edges of these plateaus, especially the eastern and the southern ones are marked by sharp mountainous walls that descend to narrow plains along the coast. There are a few broad coastal plains.

Great Atlas Mountains of Morocco

The mountains of Africa can be divided into three distinct systems:

- The Atlas Mountains
- The mountains of west coast
- The mountains of east coast

Africa is the oldest landmass in the world. Underlying the continent is an ancient block of stable crystalline rock which is more than 300 million years old!

Geography

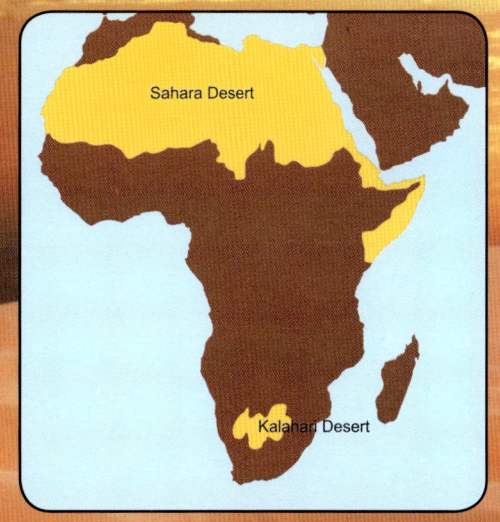

Sahara Desert

The Atlas Mountains occupy the northern portion between the Atlantic Ocean and the Mediterranean Sea and the Sahara Desert. The eastern Atlas, consist of two parallel ranges enclosing a plateau. The western Atlas Mountains are also known as the Great Atlas of Morocco.

The mountains of west coast are composed of the Cameroon Highlands and the highlands of Lower Guinea, known as the Kong Mountains.

The east coast system consists of:

- The southern section
- The section between the Zambezi and Ethiopia, containing the highest peaks in Africa and the Great Lakes. The Ethiopian system rises abruptly from the coast and gradually descends towards the Nile

Nearly one-third of the entire area of the continent is occupied by deserts. The Sahara Desert, the largest hot desert in the world, is located in northern Africa and covers 9,065,000 km^2. This is almost the size of the United States. The Sahara is a desert, not because it has a sandy surface, but due to the lack of water. Its soil, if it could be irrigated, would be highly fertile. The Kalahari in southern Africa, is another large desert.

Kalahari Desert

7

AFRICA

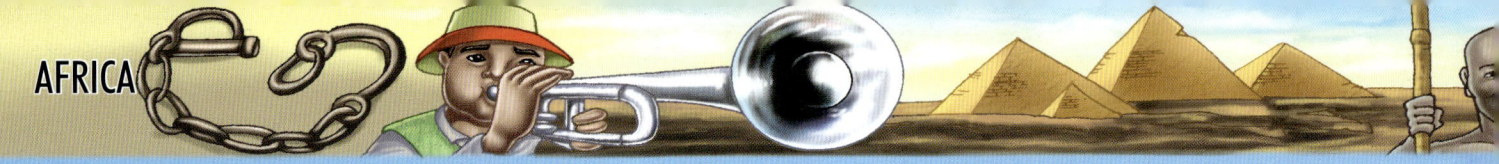

Gold

The Nile, the longest river of the world, is the most important of the African rivers. Other big rivers of Africa are the Congo, the Niger and the Zambezi. However, these rivers are commercially unimportant because of the presence of many cataracts, and lack of harbours at their mouths.

The biggest island is Madagascar, which is situated near the coast of southeast Africa. Madagascar covers 587,000 km^2.

Minerals

Africa is a rich source of minerals. Argyle diamond mine located at Kimberley, South Africa, is the richest diamond mine in the world. The richest gold mines on Earth are also located in Africa in Johannesburg.

Nile River

Climate

Kalahari Desert

A large part (almost three-fourth) of Africa lies within the tropics. This results in a year-long spell of summer with definite seasons of rain and drought. The variations in climate are caused by prevailing winds and height. The winds come from the northeast and the southeast. The north-easterly winds coming from across Asia bring no rain to northern Africa. The south-easterly winds bring moisture to coastal districts, but it falls as rain on the mountains and does not reach the interior. This resulted in the formation of the Kalahari Desert.

Since average annual temperatures are high nearly everywhere in Africa, division of the continent into climatic regions is based chiefly on amount and seasonal distribution of rainfall. Seven main types of climate affect the continent. Four are tropical, ranging from arid to extremely wet. The other three are subtropical to temperate.

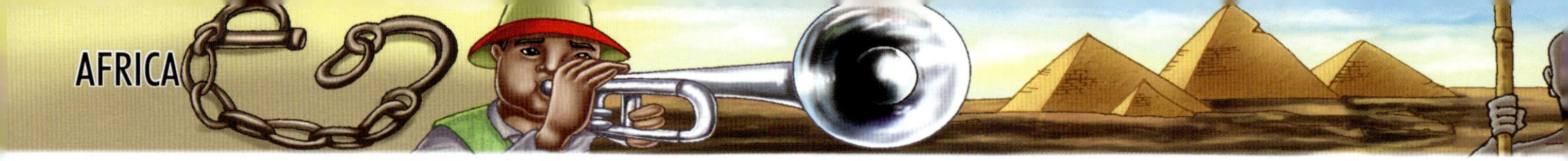

History

Early history

Africa is considered 'the birthplace of humanity'. Evidence gathered from the fossil remains found in Africa indicates that the earliest forms of humans and humanlike creatures originated here.

In eastern Africa, human remains have been found that are more than 1,500,000 years old and remains of humanlike creatures have been found that are more than 4,000,000 years old. Scientists believe that humans evolved from these humanlike creatures.

The earliest African people inhabited the Sahara region during a time when the Sahara was not a dry desert region some 10,000 years ago. There was abundant rainfall and vegetation. Many cave paintings left by them provide a record of their life and culture. When somewhere around 5000 B.C the climate of Sahara became dry and the desert began to develop the Saharan people moved away to different places and their culture disappeared.

> Scientists believe that Africa is the birthplace of human species.

History

The Pyramids of Giza

Ancient civilizations of Africa

Africa's earliest evidence of written history has been found in ancient Egypt belonging to the 4th millennium B.C., the time of the rise of the ancient Egyptian civilization. In about 3100 B.C. Egypt was united under a ruler known as Menes who inaugurated the first of the 30 dynasties into which Egypt's ancient history has been divided.

The pyramids at Giza, near Cairo, were built by the fourth dynasty. The Great Pyramid, the tomb of Pharaoh Khufu, is the only surviving monument of the Seven Wonders of the Ancient World.

Ancient Egypt was eventually overthrown by the Nubian Empire, then by the Assyrians, Persians, **Alexander the Great** and finally the Romans. The Romans colonized all of North Africa in first century B.C., spreading Christianity throughout the large areas of the region as far south as Kush and Ethiopia. However, the spread of Islam began in the late 7th century in North and East Africa leading to evolution of new cultures.

Alexander the Great

11

AFRICA

The Cape of Good Hope

Scramble for Africa

In 1652, the Dutch settled in the Cape of Good Hope area and established a link between Europe and the East on behalf of the Dutch East India Company.

The coming of explorers set in motion the process of colonization of Africa by various European countries like Belgium, Germany, Great Britain, France, Italy, Portugal and Spain that began the infamous.

The rise of Islam generated an increase in the Arab slave trade, which ended in the 19th century and eventually led to the forced transportation of slaves in the transatlantic slave trade and the beginning of European colonization throughout Africa.

The Dark Continent

For centuries Africa was known as the '**Dark Continent**' by the European world. This was because, except for the coastal regions little was known of the interior regions which were considered difficult to access due to vast deserts, dense forests and rivers that are difficult to navigate near the coast. It was only in the latter half of the 19th century did foreign explorers manage to reach deep into the interior.

> In 1487, Portuguese explorer Bartolomeu Dias became the first European to reach the southernmost tip of Africa.

Bartolomeu Dias

History

Colonisation of Africa

The setting up of a colonial empire in Africa began with the French occupation of Algeria in 1830. The Dutch, having given up the slave trade, released their Guinea stations to the British in mid-century, and in 1874 Britain declared the Gold Coast a colony. France established a partial control over Tunisia in 1881, and Britain began occupying Egypt in 1882, while Belgium took control of the Congo Basin.

Soon after, a series of wars between European colonial powers over the control of African territories ensued. The rivalry became so intense that the **Berlin Conference (1884–85)** was called to settle the disputes. Free trade was established in the Congo Basin, but most of the rest of the continent was divided into European spheres of influence.

At the Berlin Conference, most of Africa was split into areas of dominance. France and Britain got the biggest parts, and Germany, Portugal, Italy, Spain and Belgium getting small parts.

Colonialism in 1914

AFRICA

The purpose of colonisation was to extract cash crops and natural resources for the use of colonial powers. The colonists followed the policy of divide and rule to facilitate easy administration. Tribal rivalries were exploited to the advantage of the colonial powers. No attention was paid to the development of these colonies resulting in their excessive economic, cultural and social deterioration. The effects of the colonial rule was so severe that the continent has still not been able to recover from the setback.

Slave trade

Slavery had always been there in Africa since slaves were often the by-products of intertribal warfare, and the Arabs and Shirazis who dominated the East African coast took slaves in large numbers. However, it was only after the arrival of Portuguese in the 15th century that slavery was turned into a transatlantic export industry. African natives were made slaves and were transported to European and American countries.

A memorial in the former slave market in Zanzibar, Tanzania

History

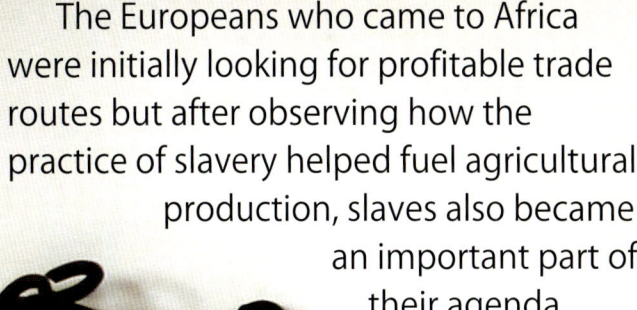

The Europeans who came to Africa were initially looking for profitable trade routes but after observing how the practice of slavery helped fuel agricultural production, slaves also became an important part of their agenda.

African tribal leaders who wanted to extend their kingdoms and become rich and powerful by waging war also aided in this transatlantic slave trade with the Europeans by providing slaves in exchange of guns.

On an approximate, from the end of the 15th century until around 1870, when the slave trade was abolished, up to 20 million Africans had been enslaved! The conditions of their transport were very inhuman and most of the slaves being transported would die during the journey. By the time slavery was abolished in the 19th century, most of the population of the continent had been wiped out.

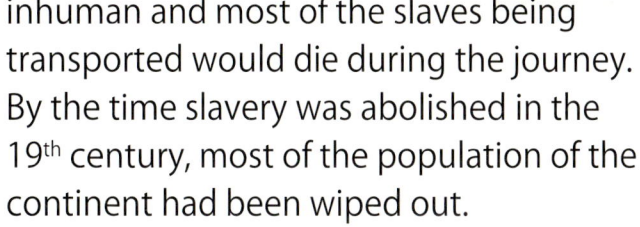

AFRICA

Independence

In 1938 there were revolts against French rule in Tunisia. The revolts were suppressed, and the leader of the revolt was imprisoned. The war broadened North Africa's contacts with the outer world and created greater restlessness. Formation of the Arab League in 1945 encouraged the Muslim countries to ask for independent rule.

The Mau Mau uprisings in Kenya in the early 1950's were one of the most violent expressions of disapproval. Libya became independent in 1951, and Eritrea joined Ethiopia in a federation in 1952. War for independence started in Tunisia in 1952.

The Algerian War began in 1954 and a revolt broke out in Morocco in 1955. Tunisia and Morocco were granted independence by France in 1956, and Algeria achieved nationhood in 1962.

Great Britain gave independence to Sudan in 1956 and Ghana in 1957. In 1958 France made Guinea an independent nation. Seventeen independent nations were created in sub-Saharan Africa by 1960.

The largest country in Africa is Sudan and the smallest country is the island nation of Seychelles.

Steve Biko was one of South Africa's most significant political activists and a leading founder of South Africa's Black Consciousness Movement. After his death in police detention in 1977 he became a martyr and a symbol of black resistance to the oppressive Apartheid regime.

Religion in Africa

The Egyptians worshipped many gods. Outside Egypt, however, the Bantu people of West Africa worshipped only one god, either the sun god or the sky god. Phoenicians and Greeks, and the Romans introduced their own gods in North Africa.

Around 300 A.D., a great change occurred in the belief systems of people of north and east Africa. People of the land converted to the faith of Christianity. By 500 A.D., Christianity spread over to most of North Africa, including Egypt, modern Sudan, Eretria and Ethiopia.

In the late 600 A.D., another faith, Islam, came to Africa. Starting from Egypt it spread rapidly across North Africa. A hundred years later, almost the entire population of North Africa had been converted to Islam. Islam quickly spread across Sahara Desert as well, so that many people of Sudan and the people living in the grasslands south of the Sahara, became Muslims as well. Due to the presence of Arabs and Indian traders, the people living on east coast of Africa became Muslim too.

Sun God

The Most Reverend Dr. Desmond Mpilo Tutu is a world famous religious leader who worked towards bringing an end to apartheid and poverty in South Africa. Bishop Desmond Tutu has been honoured with many different awards including the Nobel Peace Prize in 1984.

AFRICA

South of the rain forests, however, in central and western Africa, **Bantu** religion remained dominant. In the Kalahari Desert, the San people retained their own faith, which was very similar to the Bantu faith.

Majority of Africans are now Muslim or Christian. However, there are still a huge number of native religions practised on the continent. They share some common features—belief in one God, belief in ancestral spirits, the idea of sacrifice, often involving the death of a living thing to ensure divine protection and generosity, the need to undergo rites of passage to move from childhood to adulthood, from life to death etc.

African Muslims

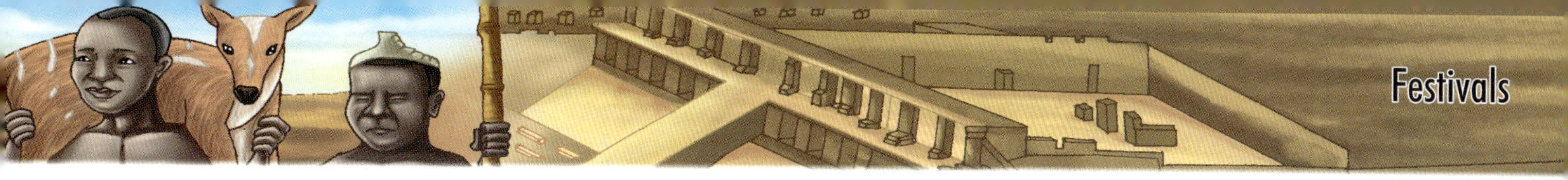

Festivals

Cape Town New Year carnival

Cape Town celebrates the New Year with great enthusiasm in the form of a carnival known as the **Minstrel Carnival**. It used to be known as the 'Coon Carnival'. The origin of the carnival dates back to the 19th century when freed slaves were given the day off on January 2nd. The parades are huge colourful affairs with grand costumes and wonderful bands which march past the crowd, singing and dancing. The competition for the best troupe is held every weekend in January.

Ramadan

Ramadan is celebrated in the ninth month of the Muslim calendar. It is considered to be the holiest month for Muslims since it was in the ninth month that Prophet Muhammad first began to receive the word of God. During the month of Ramdan, Muslims fast during the day for 30 days from dawn until sunset. During this period, Muslims abstain from food, drink and other physical needs during the daylight hours. The end of Ramadan is marked by the festival of **Eid** and the celebrations last for several days.

Minstrel Cornival

AFRICA

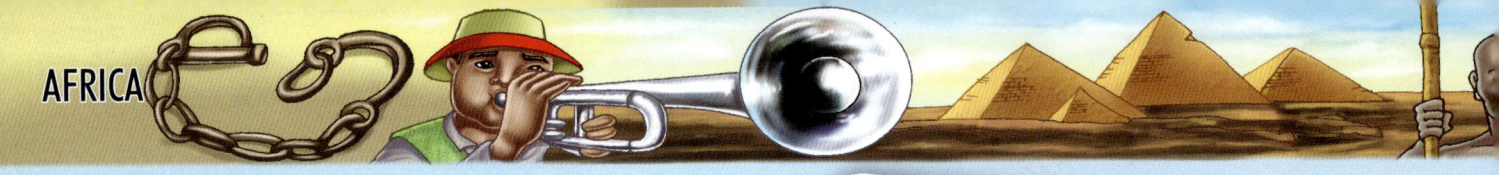

Meskel

Meskel is an old Christian festival celebrated in the month of September. It has been celebrated in Ethiopia for over 1600 years. It celebrates the discovery of the 'True Cross', the cross upon which Christ was crucified. Meskel is celebrated by dancing, feasting and lighting a massive bonfire known in Ethiopian tradition as '**Damera**'.

Damera

Meskel

Christmas

Africa is home to almost 350 million Christians. The festival of Christmas is celebrated throughout the continent. Christmas day celebrations include singing of carols, exchange of gifts, decorating Christmas tree etc.

The African people have absorbed the festival of Christmas in their own culture. They have added their own new music to the occasion and have added rhythm and chants to familiar carols that make them more meaningful to their people.

Celebrating Christmas in Africa

Kwanzaa

Kwanzaa festival was created in 1966 by Dr Maulana Ron Karenga. It lasts for seven days beginning from December 26 and ending on January 1. The name Kwanzaa means 'first fruits of the harvest' in Swahilis.

Kwanzaa

During Kwanzaa, families decorate their homes with the Kwanzaa symbols. They place a straw mat on a table, corn (one ear for each child in the family) and other foods to symbolise Earth's abundance.

There are seven basic symbols of Kwanzaa:
- Crops
- Mat
- Candle holder
- Corn
- Seven candles
- The Unity Cup
- Gifts

Candles are placed in a wooden candle holder. A black candle is placed in the centre as a reminder of the richness of African skin. Three red candles represent the struggles of the African people and three green candles represent freedom and a happy future. A candle is lit for each day of Kwanzaa.

The black candle is lit first and then red and green candles are lit alternately. After the candle lighting, families pray and offer respect to their ancestors and leaders by drinking out of the unity cup. The main feature of Kwanza is **Karamu**, the feast held on the last evening at the end of the festival. Each day during the festival people exchange gifts with each other.

There are seven principles of Kwanzaa, one for each day:
- Unity
- Self-determination
- Collective work & responsibility
- Cooperative economics
- Purpose
- Creativity
- Faith

AFRICA

New Yam Festival

New Yam Festival

New Yam Festival

The New Yam Festival is celebrated in the beginning of August at the end of the rainy season. The yam is a large tuberous root related to the sweet potato, but not exactly the same. Yams are usually the first fruits of the harvest, the staple food of many peoples of western Africa. Yams are offered to gods and ancestors and then are distributed among the villagers. This day symbolizes the conclusion of a work cycle and the beginning of another. On the last night before the festival, yams of the old year are gotten rid of by those who still have them. This is done because it is believed that the New Year must begin with tasty, fresh yams instead of the old dried-up crops of the previous year.

Incwala

Incwala or the 'festival of the first fruits,' begins at no moon when people of the Bimanti clans go to the Indian Ocean off the Mozambique coast to gather the foam of the waves which is believed to have mystical powers.

They then return to the king's royal palace and at dawn of the new moon, the king chews sacred foods prepared with the foam and spits them in the east and west. Then the festival begins.

For two days, the people wear traditional outfits and chant sacred songs while the king remains in his palace. The festival is brought to an end by burning a bonfire in which items representing the past year are burnt, followed by celebration of the new year with feasts, singing, and dancing.

Incwala

Festivals

Aboakyer

Aboakyer

It is celebrated by the people of Simpa in the Central Region of Ghana. The festival is a celebration to mark their migration from the ancient Western Sudan Empire. 'Aboakyer' translates as 'hunting for game or animal' in the Fante dialect. The people of Simpa were instructed by their traditional priest to sacrifice a young member of the Royal family every year to their god.

However, after the people made an appeal to the god, they were asked for an animal from the wild cat family to be sacrificed before the god. After they were unable to capture such an animal they made another request to their god and the god again complied by asking for a mature bush buck. The people of Simpa sang this story in their war chants and told it during moonlit nights.

The Aboakyer festival is celebrated in May each year. During the festival, two warrior groups in Winneba (Simpa) compete with each other on the first day of the festival to be the first to catch a live buck from a game reserve used for this purpose.

The winning team presents the captured buck to the chief and his sub-chiefs for a sacrifice to be made. This marks the beginning of the Aboakyer festival.

Bush Buck

Amazing Africa

Take a look at some of the most fascinating places of the continents which are evidence to Africa's rich past and row, natural beauty.

Victoria Falls

Along the boundary of Zambia and Zimbabwe, the Zambezi River falls into a jagging ravine to make the largest curtain of falling water on Earth known as the Victoria Falls. They fall from a height of 108 m and have a total width of 1,708 m.

The waterfall is known as '**Mosi oa Tunya**' (the smoke that thunders) by the locals because of the columns of spray that can be seen from miles away. Its spray is visible from a distance of 30 km and the sound of the waterfalls can be heard from a long distance.

The Victoria Falls are an unbroken cascade of water and the bottom of the abyss is obscured by a thick haze of spray and mist which is decorated by rainbows during the daytime.

Abu Simbel temples

The two temples at Abu Simbel in Egypt were built in 1257 B.C. by Pharaoh Ramses II. The temples were carved out of sandstone cliff near the west bank of the Nile near the border of Egypt with Sudan. The temples were dedicated to Ramses II and the sun gods. A statue of Ramses II is seated with three other gods within the innermost part of the temple.

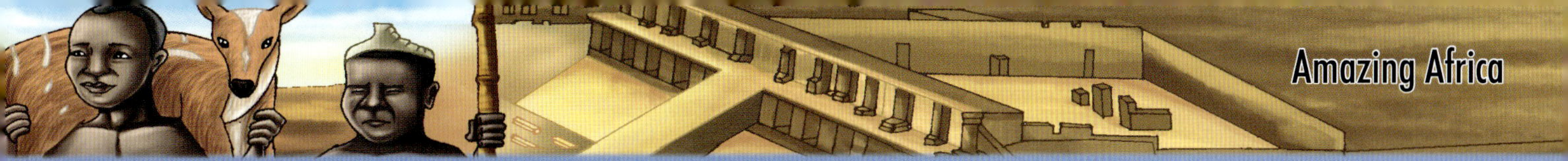

Amazing Africa

The front part of the temple is occupied by four huge seated statues of the Pharaoh (each over 20 m high). The interior of the temples consists of a series of halls and rooms. The Great Abu Simbel Temples have been so constructed that twice every year, on February 22 and October 22, the first rays of the morning sun shine down the entire length of the temple-cave illuminating the back wall of the innermost shrine and the statues of the four seated gods.

Another interesting incident associated with the temples is that they were relocated in the 1960s, when due to the construction of the Aswan High dam the temples faced the danger of being submerged under the resultant Lake, Nasser. With the assistance of UNESCO and the international community, the Egyptian government relocated the temples to an artificial mountain. The relocation involved removing the temple part by part from its earlier site and then reassembling them in exactly the same manner and in the same relationship to each other and to the sun.

Lake Nasser

AFRICA

Mt Kilimanjaro

Mt. Kilimanjaro

Popularly known as 'Kili', Mount Kilimanjaro is 5,895 m high and is the highest mountain in Africa. Mount Kilimanjaro lies on the border of Tanzania and Kenya, just south of the equator. Kilimanjaro is also the world's tallest free-standing mountain, which means its base is at the sea level. It is an extinct volcano.

The name Kilimanjaro might mean 'Mountain of Light'. However, the local people don't have a proper name for it. Among them it is known as Kipoo or Kibo.

The Great Pyramids of Giza

The Pyramids of Giza are the most famous monuments of ancient Egypt. These massive stone structures were built around 4,500 years ago on a rocky desert plateau close to River Nile near the capital city of Memphis. The Pyramids were built for the fourth dynasty kings Khufu, Khafre and Menkaure who ruled through 2589-2504 B.C.

The greatest of these pyramids is the tomb of Pharaoh Khufu (also known as Pharaoh Cheops).

Another famous monument at Giza is the great Sphinx, a half-human half-lion statue considered to be one of the world's largest and the oldest statues.

Great Sphinx

Amazing Africa

Valley of the Kings

For about 500 years (16th century B.C. to 11th century B.C.) tombs for kings and other nobles were constructed at a site near Luxor in Egypt. The site is known as the 'Valley of the Kings'. It is located on the west bank of river Nile and has 63 tombs. Most of the tombs contained priceless Egyptian artefacts most of which have been stolen. The rest have been transported to various museums.

The valley became famous after the discovery of completely preserved tomb of Tutankhamen in 1922 and is today regarded as one of the most famous archaeological sites in the world.

Valley of the Kings

Kruger National Park

Kruger National Park is the largest game reserve in South Africa. It is larger than the country of Israel. The total area of the reserve is 20,000 km² from north to south along the Mozambique border. The Park has been rated as the ultimate safari experience.

The National Park was opened in 1898 at the instigation of then President of South Africa, Paul Kruger. After poachers had damaged the originally rich game stock to a severe extent, all the land between the Sabie and the Crocodile Rivers was put under the protection of Nature Conservation to ensure the survival of the remaining animals. Only as recently as 1961 was the extended Kruger Park fenced in.

Kruger National Park is home to a large number of species of trees, fish, amphibians, reptiles, birds and mammals.

AFRICA

Ngorongoro Crater

Ngorongoro Crater

The Ngorongoro Crater is the world's largest unbroken, volcanic caldera. It is about 19 km wide, 600 m deep from the rim of the crater to its floor with a total floor area of 260 km².

The crater is the result of a huge volcanic explosion which happened approximately three million years ago. After the explosion the volcano collapsed on itself. Ngorongoro crater is considered to be a natural enclosure for wildlife, with many animal species being found on the crater floor.

The Virunga Mountains

The Virunga Mountains are a range of volcanic mountains on the borders of Uganda, Rwanda and the Democratic Republic of Congo (DRC). The forests of the Virunga Mountains are the only remaining homes of the endangered mountain gorillas. Other interesting animals found there include Chimpanzees, the Okapi and forest elephants.

Virunga Mountains

Mountain Gorillas

Amazing Africa

Table Mountain

Table Mountain

Table Mountain is a mountain in the Western Cape, South Africa, overlooking the greater Cape Town area. It forms part of the Table Mountain National Park and is bordered by Devil's Peak in the east and by Lion's Head and Signal Hill in the north.

Table Mountain is a famous landmark and tourist attraction in Cape Town, with many visitors using the aerial cableway to take a ride to the top. The mountain is named for its flat top which is often covered by cloud, forming a sort of 'table cloth'. Views from the top are excellent on a clear day. It stands 1,086 m above sea level. Table Mountain is a national icon and it features on the flag of Cape Town.

Fish River Canyon

Regarded as the second most spectacular canyon in the world (after the Grand Canyon of America), the Fish River Canyon is indeed a sight of astonishing grandeur.

The canyon features a 160 km narrow valley which is up to 27 km wide and 550 m in some places. The Fish River flows through the valley.

Fish River Canyon

29

Famous people

Wangari Maathai

A famous environmentalist and human rights activist from Kenya, Wangari Maathai is well-known for the 'Green Belt Movement'. She has inspired people worldwide, to take up the cause of afforestation. She is the first African woman to receive the Nobel Prize in 2004 for her efforts.

Nelson Mandela

One of the greatest leaders of the 20th century, Nelson Mandela worked to free his nation from apartheid (discrimination between people on the basis of colour). He was awarded the Nobel Prize in 1993. On May 10, 1994, Nelson Mandela became the President of South Africa and completed his term in 1999. He was the first President to have been elected democratically in the history of South Africa.

Albert John Luthuli

He was the first African to be awarded a Nobel Prize for Peace (1960), in recognition of his non-violent struggle against racial discrimination. He led ten million black Africans in their non-violent campaign for the civil rights in South Africa.

Akinwande Oluwole 'Wole' Soyinka

Wole Soyinka, Nigerian was a playwright and political activist who received the Nobel Prize for Literature in 1986. He was the first African to be awarded the Nobel Prize for Literature.

Test Your MEMORY

1. How many countries does Africa have?
2. What is the highest point in Africa?
3. Name the body of land connecting Asia and Africa?
4. Who was the first European to reach Africa and when?
5. When was Berlin Conference held?
6. Who created the Kwanza Festival?
7. What are the seven symbols of the Kwanzaa Festival?
8. What is yam?
9. What is the other name for Victoria Falls?
10. What is the Great Sphinx?
11. Who is the first African woman to be awarded the Nobel Prize?
12. Who is the first African to be award the Nobel Prize?

Index

A

Africa 3, 4, 5, 6, 7, 8, 9, 10, 11, 12, 13, 14, 15, 16, 17, 18, 20, 22, 26, 27, 29, 30
apartheid 16, 17, 30

C

caldera 28
cave paintings 10
Christianity 11, 17
civilization 11
climate 3, 9, 10
coastline 6
colonial 13, 14
colonization 12
continent 3, 4, 5, 6, 7, 9, 12, 13, 14, 15, 18, 20

D

Damera 20
desert 3, 7, 9, 10, 12, 17, 18, 26
drought 9

E

Earth 3, 6, 8, 21, 24
empire 11, 13, 23
equator 3, 5, 26

extinct volcano 26

F

festivals 19, 21
fossil 10

G

gods 17, 22, 24, 25

H

highest 4, 7, 26
highlands 7
history 10, 11, 30
humanity 10

I

independent 16
Islam 11, 12, 17
island 4, 5, 8
Isthmus 5

L

landmass 6
largest 3, 4, 6, 7, 24, 26, 27, 28
longest 3, 4, 8
lowest 4

M

minerals 8

mountains 6, 7, 9, 28

P

peninsulas 6
Pharaoh 11, 24, 25, 26
physical 6, 19
plateaus 6
pyramids 11, 26

R

racial discrimination 30
rain 9, 18
Ramdan 19
ranges 7
religion 17, 18
revolts 16
rivers 8, 12, 27

S

safari 27
slave 12, 13, 14, 15
slavery 14, 15
summer 9

T

tribe 4

V

valley 27, 29
Victoria Falls 24

* Maps not to scale; for illustration purpose only.